BRITISH RAILWAYS

PAST and PRESENT

No 19

South West Scotland

Keith Sanders & Douglas Hodgins

Past and Present

Past & Present Publishing Ltd

First published in October 1993
New edition with colour February 1995
Reprinted September 1999

British Library Cataloguing in Publication Data

A catalogue record for this book is available from the British Library

ISBN 1 85895 074 0

Past & Present Publishing Ltd
The Trundle
Ringstead Road
Great Addington
Kettering
Northants
NN14 4BW

Tel/Fax: 01536 330588
email: sales@slinkp-p.demon.co.uk

NOTE: All the 'present' photos have been taken by Keith Sanders; the picture credits refer to the photographers of the 'past' views. All research and captions are by Douglas Hodgins.

Maps drawn by Christina Siviter

Printed and bound in Great Britain

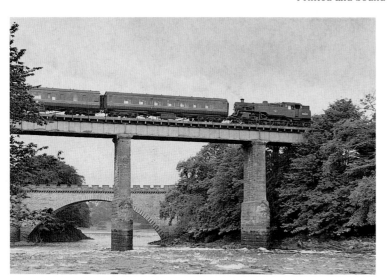

TONGLAND BRIDGE: This 1963 view of the Kirkcudbright branch shows Standard tank No 80023 crossing the River Dee at Tongland Bridge shortly after leaving the terminus for Castle Douglas. The roadbridge in the background was built by Thomas Telford in 1805. *Michael Mensing*

In 1993 it can be seen that there has been minimal change apart from the removal of the bridge girders. The road bridge is now carrying much more traffic than was ever anticipated when it was built. (See also pages 74-78)

CONTENTS

BIBLIOGRAPHY

Legends of the Glasgow & South Western Railway *by David L. Smith (David & Charles)*
BR Steam Motive Power Depots, Scottish Region *by Paul Bolger (Ian Allan)*
Scottish Branch Line Steam *by Jack Kernahan (Bradford Barton)*
LMS Engine Sheds, Volume 5, The Caledonian Railway *by Chris Hawkins and George Reeve (Wild Swan)*
  Volume 7, The Glasgow & South Western Railway *by Chris Hawkins, George Reeve and James Stevenson (Irwell Press)*

Forgotten Railways - Scotland *by John Thomas (David & Charles)*
A Regional History of the Railways of Great Britain, Volume 6, Scotland - The Lowlands and The Borders *by John Thomas (David & Charles)*
Encyclopaedia of British Railway Companies *by Christopher Awdry (Patrick Stephens Limited)*
Jowett's Atlas of Great Britain and Ireland *by Alan Jowett (Patrick Stephens Limited)*
The Handbook of Steam Motive Power Depots, Volume 4, Northern England and Scotland *by Paul Smith (Platform 5)*

BEATTOCK SUMMIT: Stanier '5MT' No 44764, fitted with Timken roller bearings, powers 1M97 past the summit signal box on 1 August 1964, while a Fairburn 2-6-4T stands on the down line waiting to cross over and return to Beattock MPD. The large board on the front of the signal box was a feature of the spot. *Rodney Lissenden*

Although the summit signal box has long been demolished, the spot is still marked by a board proclaiming that the line is 1,015 feet above sea level and the location is 52 miles from Glasgow and 349 miles from London. An HST rushes past the board on 22 June 1993 with an Edinburgh-Penzance working. How many passengers would have noticed the sign?

INTRODUCTION

Welcome to South West Scotland and LMS territory. At the Grouping in 1923, all the railways in the area covered were worked by the Glasgow & South Western Railway (G&SWR), the Caledonian Railway (CR) or jointly. The G&SWR had all the area west of the Gretna Green-Dumfries-Kilmarnock line, which included the Ayrshire coalfield lines. The CR was represented by the West Coast Main Line and branches, Lanarkshire and the suburban lines of South Glasgow. The Caley did manage to stray as far west as Wemyss Bay and Ardrossan.

The route from Kilmarnock through Barrhead, to just south of the Clyde, was a joint line, as was the 'Port Road' from Castle Douglas to Portpatrick. This latter line was actually the Portpatrick & Wigtownshire Joint Railway, which was owned by the LNWR, MR, G&SWR and CR, but the running of it was left to the two Scottish companies.

On my visits to the area I found that the 'Port Road' had a lot of similarities to the Waverley Route. It was an undulating line which passed through two reasonably sized towns and crossed some wild moorland. For the most part the railway had just been removed and the trackbed handed back to nature. Only in the towns of Castle Douglas and Newton Stewart have there been any trackbed developments. In the same way that Shankend Viaduct still stands on the Waverley, so Big Water of Fleet Viaduct is to be found intact on the 'Port Road', a large reminder of the railway age in an otherwise desolate moorland. Knowing that the railway had gone, it was sad to see the volume of road-transported freight being loaded on to the ferries at Stranraer.

Some symbols of the old railway exist, however. There are still semaphore signals at Stranraer, and also at Thornhill, Kirkconnel and New Cumnock on the G&SWR main line. The coal sub-sector of Railfreight is in residence at Ayr, but the volume of traffic is but a shadow of what used to be hauled by the 'Crab' 2-6-0s in the 'fifties.

The one area of intensive activity was the Glasgow suburban lines where, thanks to Strathclyde PTE support, there were frequent passenger services running.

The West Coast Main Line had all the expense of electrification many years ago, but because of the amount of freight business lost by the railways, the line is now used to nowhere near its capacity. Closure of the traditional heavy industries such as the Ravenscraig Steelworks has meant the loss of substantial revenue for the railways. Gone is the transport of iron ore and coal as the raw materials, and also gone is the transporting of the end product - sad times.

Nevertheless I have enjoyed doing the book, and thanks must go to the photographers who supplied the 'past' pictures, to the landowners who readily granted permission to go on their property to obtain the 'present' pictures, to my co-author for the research, to Donald Cameron for the loan of old maps, and to my wife Barbara for encouraging me to undertake my second volume and for proof-reading the manuscript.

Finally, to prove that there is still life in me, I am now off across the Clyde to do the North West Scotland volume!

Keith Sanders
Longniddry

The West Coast Main Line

The Caledonian Railway opened the line from Carlisle to Glasgow on 15 February 1848 and from Carstairs to Edinburgh (Princes Street) on the same day. The Caledonian offered a direct service from London to Glasgow or Edinburgh without changing whereas passengers using the East Coast route had to make two changes on the journey north, at Newcastle and Berwick. The Post Office quickly switched its mail train to the West Coast route in March 1848, and on 1 May that year the first express passenger train ran between London and Glasgow/Edinburgh. This service was followed by express trains linking the two major Scottish cities with Manchester, Liverpool and Birmingham. Passengers flocked to use the new services linking Scotland with the south and many excursion trains were run at very low fares.

Livestock trains followed as the farming community saw the advantages of moving animals south to the markets in a matter of hours rather than making the long road journey. Many branches sprouted from the main line. The Solway Junction Railway opened over the 20 miles from Kirtlebridge to Brayton using the Solway Viaduct, which was over a mile in length; the purpose of the line was to move iron ore from the mines in Cumberland to the Lanarkshire steelworks. The Solway Viaduct proved costly to maintain and repair, but the ore traffic fell away and the viaduct was condemned in 1921.

In September 1863 a line from Lockerbie to Dumfries was opened, followed in 1883 by the short branch from Beattock to Moffat. In 1901 a branch from near Elvanfoot to Leadhills was added; a year later it was extended to Wanlockhead. Further north, at Symington, a line was opened to Peebles in 1864. Carstairs was, and still is, an important junction, where the line to Edinburgh diverges from the Glasgow line. A line to Dolphinton was opened in 1867 but prior to this, on 5 January 1855, the Lanark Railway was running trains from Cleghorn to Lanark.

From June 1878 it was possible to travel from Ayr to Edinburgh via Muirkirk and Carstairs, but it was a slow journey and never popular. North of Carstairs the railway passed through industrial Lanarkshire on its way to Glasgow with many lines branching from the main line to places such as Coatbridge, Wishaw, Hamilton and Coalburn. The coming of the railway to industrial Lanarkshire caused a great influx of people to the area and small villages saw a tenfold increase in population in the space of a few years.

Today there is not one branch line between Carlisle and Carstairs and only Lockerbie station remains open. In Lanarkshire most of the heavy industry has gone and with it the freight traffic, but the area is well served by a frequent service of suburban electrics to Glasgow.

QUINTINSHILL: 'Jubilee' No 45671 *Prince Rupert* is seen at speed with the 9.30 am Manchester-Glasgow express on 26 August 1956, passing Quintinshill, scene of the horrific railway disaster of 1915 which cost so many lives. *Robert Leslie*

There is not a great deal of change from the past picture as a Class '86' heads north with a down express on 21 June 1993, except of course the line is now electrified using the 25KV overhead system. The loops have been lengthened, but the old signal box in the distance together with the semaphore signals have gone. The growth of the tree on the right-hand side has necessitated a more head-on viewpoint.

9

KIRKPATRICK FLEMING: The first of the three views of this attractive location (opposite) depicts ex-LMS 'Pacific' No 46223 *Princess Alice* with the Sunday up 'Royal Scot' on 24 August 1958. *Robert Leslie*

The second view is of unnamed 'Britannia' No 70047 with a Glasgow-Birmingham train on 4 June 1960. The lack of exhaust means that the signal box and station buildings can be seen quite clearly. *Gavin W. Morrison*

The present day, and on a sunny 21 June 1993 No 86253 *The Manchester Guardian* heads for Carlisle with an up train. The layout has been simplified over the years and in this instance fewer, not more, trees reveal the former goods yard and the large school building beyond. The goods yard is used by an agricultural engineering firm and presents a rather untidy appearance. Part of the low retaining wall can be seen behind the 25KV stanchion. The local tourist attraction is Robert the Bruce's cave.

KIRTLEBRIDGE: A Liverpool-Glasgow express heads north behind 'Jubilee' No 45674 *Duncan* on 24 August 1958. To the south of the station was the junction for the Solway Junction line to Cumbria (Cumberland), which opened in 1869 for goods traffic, and to passengers the following year; in 1895 it passed into the ownership of the Caledonian Railway. The line crossed the Solway Firth on a viaduct 1,940 yards long and supported on 193 piers. From the start there were problems with the viaduct and as a result of lack of maintenance during the First World War it was closed to traffic in 1921 and demolished in about 1934. *Robert Leslie*

A visit to the location on 21 June 1993 provided a northbound HST. All the signals, box, station and sidings have gone, giving way to a simple double-track main line. The A74 road is in the top left of the pictures; its widening to a dual carriageway necessitated the demolition of some of the houses in the 'past' shot. It is interesting to note that the railway boundary fence still follows the line of the old goods yard.

LOCKERBIE: Preserved GNSR 4-4-0 No 49 *Gordon Highlander* was photographed on 13 June 1959, working an SLS Special from Glasgow (St Enoch) to Lockerbie, Dumfries and Kilmarnock and back to St Enoch. *David A. Anderson*

The buildings in the background have hardly changed over the years, with the Town Hall clock tower continuing to dominate the skyline. The large building on the right is now partly obscured by a large tree as No 86255 *Penrith Beacon* departs with an Edinburgh-Liverpool train on 21 June 1993. The extensive sidings are used by the Permanent Way Department, as evidenced by the two Plasser tampers.

BEATTOCK: These three views are looking south from the road bridge north of the station. On 15 May 1960, Standard Class '5' 4-6-0 No 73100 restarts a northbound freight after taking on a banker. *Robert Leslie*

On 24 June 1966 'Black Five' No 45126 heads north being banked by No 76098. This telephoto shot shows the MPD and signal box more clearly. There is little activity in the shed yard as it was only to remain open until the following year. *Roger Siviter*

The present view, taken on 22 June 1993, shows No 90025, in Railfreight Distribution livery, heading towards the site of the former station, shed and signal box. These have all gone, to be replaced by overhead wires, while the sidings are used by the Permanent Way Department. The Moffat branch swung away from the main line beyond the bridge from which the photographs were taken.

BEATTOCK MPD (68D): The main purpose of the depot was to provide engines for banking duties on northbound trains up the stiff climb to Beattock summit. The two-road shed also provided the motive power for the short Moffat branch until the latter closed on 6 April 1964. The shed lasted until the end of steam in Scotland in May 1967, when the few remaining locomotives were taken away for scrapping.

Over the years Beattock shed played host to some interesting classes. Prior to 1953 much of the banking work was performed by Pickersgill 4-6-2Ts, seven of which arrived at the shed just after the Second World War. These were replaced by Fairburn and Standard 2-6-4Ts, and there was even a brief visit from two Fowler 2-6-2Ts, but these were not liked by the crews and soon returned south. Here we see Fairburn 2-6-4Ts Nos 42192 and 42205 with Caley 0-4-4T No 55234 posing in the sun on 20 May 1961.
Gavin W. Morrison

The site retains two rarely used sidings and on 22 June 1993 there was no trace of any shed building. To think that this spot used to be a hive of activity with the banking engines, but today northbound trains sweep past as if Beattock bank no longer existed!

MOFFAT: The railway reached Moffat on 2 April 1883 by means of a branch line from Beattock station. The branch was under 2 miles in length but it helped to bring many summer visitors to the town and for a time it had its own train to Glasgow - 'The Tinto Express'. The photograph shows Standard 2-6-4T No 80118 in the station with a rail-tour on 29 March 1964, eight days before the closure of the line. *Rodney Lissenden*

Although surrounded by bushes and pallets, the station building and platform still survived intact on 22 June 1993. The building is in an excellent state of repair, being used by the local Council to store equipment used for maintaining the beautiful gardens beyond the building. The station yard has a warehouse built upon it which is used by an animal feedstuffs supplier.

GRESKINE: The northbound ascent of Beattock was particularly strenuous, hence the provision of a loop on the down side, operated by Greskine box at the northern end. 'Black Five' No 45364, fitted with snowplough and being banked in the rear, passes the end of the loop on 9 October 1963 with a lengthy freight train. *Hugh Ballantyne*

The scene today is no longer recognisable as the same location. The loop, box, signals and pole route have all gone, and the trees have grown up on both sides of the line to provide an avenue of greenery. Nowadays trains climb the incline with little effort, as demonstrated by this HST on 24 June 1993.

HARTHOPE FARM (I): This location is to the south of the viaduct by which the line crosses the A74 road. English Electric Type 4 No D374 heads a down express from the south on 1 August 1964. At this date steam was still much in evidence - note that the heavy train is being banked in the rear by a steam loco - but the diesel classes were beginning to intrude more and more. *Rodney Lissenden*

The location is immediately recognisable today, although there have been changes. The hilltops are now forested, but thanks to the removal of some trees the background farm is more visible. No 86207 *City of Lichfield* speeds up the bank unaided on 24 June 1993.

HARTHOPE FARM (2): Another diesel, English Electric Type 1 No D8078, runs down Beattock bank with an up freight on the same day. *Rodney Lissenden*

On 24 June 1993 an Aberdeen-Plymouth HST is seen heading south. The A74 is still visible in the background but the main change is the forest on the hilltops. It is interesting to note that whilst the diesel class in the 'past' picture was relatively new in 1964, very few remain in service in 1993.

HARTHOPE VIADUCT: The busy A74 trunk road follows the railway all the way from Beattock village to the summit of the line, and at Harthope the line crosses over it on a large metal viaduct, visible here at the rear of the train, together with a very quiet A74. Class '5' No 45088, with a 2-6-4T banking, heads a northbound freight on 15 May 1960. In those days lots of goods went by rail with relatively little by road. *Robert Leslie*

Because of the vast increase in road traffic, the A74 was later made into a dual carriageway and realigned, leaving the road in the 'past' picture as a lay-by; the road is currently being upgraded to a motorway (M74). On 24 June 1993 the viaduct is barely visible because of the bushes as No 90005 *Financial Times* rushes past with the 06.20 from London Euston to Glasgow. The railway has moved its boundary fence closer to the running lines and the land is now heavy undergrowth. Note the extent of the forest in the background.

ELVANFOOT: 'Jubilee' No 45661 *Vernon* pulls away from Elvanfoot station with an afternoon Carlisle-Glasgow (Central) stopping train on 11 April 1960. *David A. Anderson*

Thirty-three years later almost to the day, on the modern electrified railway No 90013 heads a down express on 7 April 1993. The trappings of the steam age - the pole route, signals and station - have all gone, the bridge has received a new parapet but the sleeper fence still survives, albeit at a slightly more jaunty angle. The Leadhills and Wanlockhead branch left the main line half a mile to the north of the station.

ABINGTON (1): On a dreary 8 October 1963 No 72009 *Clan Stewart* rolls into Abington station with a stopping train for Glasgow. The station nameboard clearly indicates that passengers for Leadhills and Wanlockhead should change here (Abington was the last station in the up direction before the branch left the main line between there and Elvanfoot). *Hugh Ballantyne*

There is no longer a station at Abington, so the opportunity was taken to extend the loops further south as can be seen in the picture of a Class '90' heading north on a freight on 7 April 1993. The road and overbridge remain, albeit with different fences and parapet, but the absence of the station footbridge meant that a slightly different viewpoint had to be used.

ABINGTON (2): 'Crab' 2-6-0 No 42737 produces a fine smoke effect with a railtour on 29 March 1964 as it approaches Abington station from the north. *Rodney Lissenden*

While there have been the usual electrification and signalling changes, the location is still recognisable as a Class '86' passes with an up express. Most of the sleeper fence has disappeared, but remains of it can still be seen at the rear of the train.

CARSTAIRS (1): Rebuilt 'Patriot' No 45527 *Southport* arrives at Carstairs with the Manchester/Liverpool Sleeper on 14 May 1960. The Manchester and Liverpool portions were combined at Preston and the train will now be split into Glasgow and Edinburgh portions. The 'Patriot' will then continue with the Glasgow portion (usually the front) while a second loco will couple on the rear to form the Edinburgh portion. The 'Patriots' were the least common of the ex-LMS passenger locomotives in Scotland, especially the unrebuilt variety which only appeared on occasional summer specials. *Michael Mensing*

On 31 May 1993 No 90011 *The Chartered Institute of Transport* hurries past on the through lines with an express for Glasgow. The scene is now uncluttered by sidings and wagons and the track layout rationalised.

CARSTAIRS (2): Seen from a slightly different viewpoint, an ex-LMS 2-6-4T heads out of the south end of the station with the Edinburgh portion of a train from Birmingham. This 1960s scene was re-enacted many times as trains to/from the south were joined/split at Carstairs. *Michael Mensing*

The same scene on 31 May 1993 shows an Edinburgh-West of England train departing south after reversing at the station. As the line to Edinburgh is now electrified, most West Coast line trains run straight past, avoiding the station completely. The track layout is much simplified as a result, with a ladder crossing making the diamond crossings but a memory.

CARSTAIRS (3): Looking into the station, under a threatening sky, Motherwell-based 'Black Five' No 45484 heads south with a mixed freight. In the platform road stands McIntosh Caledonian '3F' No 57604 which was a Carstairs engine at the time. The MPD building is on the right of the picture; it was coded 66E, having changed from 64D. Note the magnificent gantry of semaphore signals. *Michael Mensing*

The modern scene shows a Mk 4 DVT leading a Glasgow/Edinburgh-King's Cross train which was making an additional Bank Holiday stop at Carstairs on 31 May 1993. The engine shed and gantry have gone and the track-work simplified, but the station canopy has been extended.

CARSTAIRS (4): The Glasgow end of the station sees 'Jubilee' No 45673 *Keppel* heading past the Permanent Way Depot on 16 August 1958 with a stopping train from Carlisle. Note again another magnificent gantry and the lattice Caledonian signal posts. *David A. Anderson*

The loss of the semaphores and the addition of the overhead wires are the main changes as No 86241 *Glenfiddich* runs into the station with a southbound train. There has been virtually no change to the track layout.

CARSTAIRS (5): Again looking into the station, a superb study of Caledonian '2P' 0-4-4T No 55261, the Carstairs station pilot, shunting stock on 17 September 1956. *David A. Anderson*

The signal box and the semaphores have all gone to be replaced by colour light signals controlled by Motherwell power box. The houses in the background are unchanged, albeit partially obscured by the overhead line apparatus in this view of No 86204 *City of Carlisle* on a down train on 31 May 1993.

LANARK JUNCTION: 'Black Five' No 45173 passes Lanark Junction with an up goods on 15 April 1961, a typical scene with tidy embankments, semaphore signals, signal box and pole route. *W. A. C. Smith*

By way of contrast all the aforementioned items have gone in the present-day view of No 87002 *Royal Sovereign* hauling an up express on 23 May 1993. In addition, the eastern spur of the triangle has been removed and a bungalow now stands on the former trackbed where the '20' sign used to be. The west spur to Lanark is beyond the bungalow.

LAW JUNCTION: At one time this was a large station, even boasting some carriage sidings. The 'past' picture shows 'Jubilee' No 45715 *Invincible* leaving with the 2.15 pm train from Glasgow (Central) to Lanark on 19 March 1955. *W. A. C. Smith*

The modern scene on 24 June 1993 shows the typical rationalisation that has taken place as a Mk 3 DVT heads the 17.00 to London Euston with No 87028 *Lord President* propelling at the rear. The station and carriage sidings have all gone, leaving a fairly simple layout. The lines to Wishaw and Mossend diverge to the right with the Glasgow lines to the left; the foreground line leads to an Isis Link parcels depot which appears to be closed.

MOTHERWELL, LESMAHAGOW JUNCTION: Fairburn 2-6-4T No 42217 passes the junction on its run into Motherwell station with the 5.43 pm Glasgow (Central) to Symington service on 29 June 1960, while a 'Black Five' waits at the signals with a freight from the Mossend direction. *W. A. C. Smith*

The same spot on 1 August 1993 sees EMU No 314206 leaving the station with a service for Glasgow (Central) via Bellshill. The trackwork has been rationalised over the years and all the diamond crossings have been eliminated. The platforms have been extended northwards and the overhead wires and masts dominate the view. Most of the buildings on the right have been demolished, although the church has survived. On the left the factory of Motherwell Bridge and Engineering Company remains in use.

MOTHERWELL MPD (66B): The shed at Motherwell opened in 1866, and the main duties of the depot's locomotives were to serve the local coalfields and steelworks. The depot always had a large allocation of mainly goods engines and on Sundays upwards of 100 locos could be found on shed. The giant Mossend yard nearby required a large number of locos for the many freight trains and the giant Ravenscraig steel complex also generated substantial traffic. Steam managed to survive at 66B until May 1967 when the depot's last few locos were withdrawn.

The first diesels had begun to arrive at Motherwell in 1956, and the 'past' picture, taken on 18 April 1966, shows English Electric Type 1 No D8119 sitting outside the shed. The '20s', as this class later became known, have only a few survivors and none are in Scotland. *Noel A. Machell*

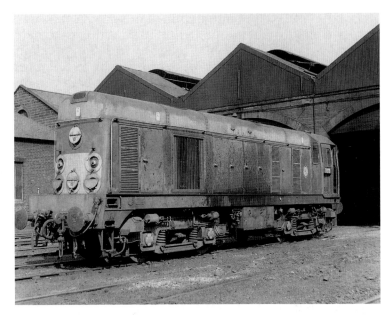

The shed survives to this day as a diesel depot, albeit re-roofed, although with the closure of Ravenscraig and the coalfields there is little work for its locomotives. However, a reasonable number of differing diesel classes can usually be found in and around the shed. A general view of the depot on 1 August 1993 shows No 37424 *Isle of Mull* in a similar position to the '20'. No 47200 is also visible on the extreme left. An exact view was not possible as permission to access the depot for this purpose was denied.

Polmadie MPD (66A), situated in south-east Glasgow (see the map on page 136), was a vast complex which opened in 1875 and was rebuilt during the 1920s. The depot was modernised further in 1941 and was the Caledonian Railway's largest shed. Its workings were varied, with passenger turns to Edinburgh, Gourock, Wemyss Bay, the Cathcart Circle and of course to Carlisle. There were also many coal and goods workings covered by the shed.

The 14-road shed had an allocation in excess of 150 locos and a Sunday visit could produce some 200 locos. Many were the classes shedded at Polmadie, but pride of place went to the fleet of 'Coronation' Class 'Pacifics', closely followed by the 'Royal Scot' 4-6-0s, and latterly the 'Britannia' and 'Clan' 'Pacifics'. Towards the end of steam Polmadie was allocated some LNER 'A2' Class 'Pacifics', but they were disliked by the crews and saw little work.

Summer Saturday mornings spent on the Polmadie Road overbridge at the rear of the shed, overlooking the main line, were extremely hectic. Between 9.00 am and 11.00 am the place was a hive of activity as a procession of locos came off shed and backed down to Glasgow (Central) to pick up their trains. After a suitable time had elapsed, the locos appeared once more with their respective trains heading south, and by the time they passed Polmadie they were well into their stride. A path from the road bridge led to the back of the shed and provided an unofficial entrance for spotters.

The 1960s heralded the invasion of the diesels, and the last Polmadie steam working took place on 28 May 1967, although visiting steam engines from other depots appeared for several months after this date. The shed continued as a diesel depot for many years before being demolished and the site turned over to a carriage depot.

POLMADIE MPD (1): Two of the LNER intruders are seen at the Polmadie Road end of Glasgow's premier depot on 18 April 1965, with No 60535 *Hornets Beauty* **nearest the camera; it is suspected that the other Peppercorn 'Pacific' in the shot is No 60527** *Sun Chariot*. **According to records, these two locos, together with Nos 60530** *Sayajirao*, **60512** *Steady Aim* **and 60522** *Straight Deal*, **were allocated to Polmadie with effect from 15 September 1963. However, Nos 60530 and 60512 had been transferred to Dundee at the time of this picture with the remaining three stored out of use and being dispatched for scrapping later in 1965. Being LNER engines they did not find favour amongst the LMS men and saw very little use whilst at Polmadie.** *Noel A. Machell*

The picture taken on 1 August 1993 shows that the main shed building has been demolished, but the brick building on the left survives, minus its chimney and with the upstairs windows bricked up. The large building in the background retains its distinctive ventilators - in steam days this was the repair depot.

POLMADIE MPD (2): Stanier 'Pacific' No 46222 *Queen Mary* stands at the east end of the shed alongside Fairburn 2-6-4T No 42057 on 16 September 1962. This side of the shed (nearest the main line) was 'reserved' for passenger locos, while freight locos were relegated to the far side. *Noel A. Machell*

Following the demolition of the large shed building the site is now a staff car park and carriage sidings. Thanks are due to John Little, Supervisor at Polmadie, for his assistance in identifying the exact location of the picture.

POLMADIE: Grubby 'Black Five' No 44668, one of ten examples fitted with Skefko roller bearings on the driving coupled axle, approaches Polmadie MPD with a freight train from the Glasgow direction on 27 June 1957. *Brian Morrison*

Thirty-six years later a Mk 3 DVT forms the rear of an ECS working to Glasgow (Central) on 1 August 1993. The nearer factory on the left survives, but the one on the right has been demolished together with its chimneys. It is ironic that the existence of modern industrial units on the north side of the line prevented an exactly duplicated viewpoint.

EGLINTON STREET: Situated within a mile of Glasgow (Central) station, the platforms at Eglinton Street were an excellent vantage point to watch trains. The first picture shows the up 'Royal Scot' gathering speed behind diesel-electrics Nos 10201 and 10202 on 2 February 1957. *W. A. C. Smith*

Today the station has gone completely. On 24 July 1993 the only distinctive feature to connect this view with the upper one opposite is the wall on the right-hand side - the two ex-Southern diesels would have been on the far right track of the pair of lines used today as relief lines for ECS movements between Central and Polmadie. The 'CAPSTAN' advertisement on the bridge above the third coach of the 'Royal Scot' has been replaced by one advertising 'TOA TAXIS', and the old tenements by high-rise flats which in turn are being replaced by low-rise housing - examples of each are to be seen in the pictures. The large high-rise flats on the right of the present-day picture are in the Gorbals district of Glasgow. EMU No 303004 is heading out on the Cathcart lines, while the 'Sprinter' is heading into Central on the West Coast Main Line.

The third picture, on the west side of the station, depicts McIntosh Caledonian 0-4-4T No 55819 rolling into the suburban platforms with the 5.39 pm Cathcart Inner Circle train from Glasgow (Central) on 8 September 1955. Note the Caledonian route indicator on the bunker. This loco is preserved by the Scottish Railway Preservation Society at Bo'ness as CR No 419. *W. A. C. Smith*

The G&SWR route

GRETNA GREEN: The up 'Thames Clyde Express', headed by 'Royal Scot' No 46103 *Royal Scots Fusilier*, passes Gretna Green station on 2 March 1958. *Robert Leslie*

The section between Gretna and Annan is now single line, but becomes double track again through the site of the old station prior to joining the West Coast Main Line at Gretna Junction. A 'Sprinter' on a Carlisle-bound service on 21 June 1993 passes the up-side station building which is now a private dwelling house; the down-side building, platform and sidings have long gone. However, it is not all closure and rationalisation as in the background can be seen a new station platform under construction.

EASTRIGGS: Situated between Gretna Junction and Annan is the village of Eastriggs; the main employer in the area being the Ministry of Defence Depot, ESD Eastriggs. The 'past' picture shows a view of the station and goods yard as they were on 24 May 1959, with Standard Class '5' No 73063 and 'Royal Scot' No 46145 *The Duke of Wellington's Regt (West Riding)* working the up 'Thames Clyde Express'. *Robert Leslie*

Looking at the location today, the station, goods yard and pole route have all gone, the track has been singled and the down-side station building is a private house. On 24 June 1993 No 37298 is seen with a trip working of containers from ESD Eastriggs to Carlisle. No longer do crack expresses thunder by, the most prestigious train today being the four-coach 'Sprinter' on the Newcastle-Stranraer service!

ANNAN: 'Jubilee' 4-6-0 No 45697 *Achilles* heads the Sunday 9.25 am Glasgow (St Enoch)-London (St Pancras) train away from Annan on 26 August 1956. In the background is the bridge that carried the Solway Junction line from Kirtlebridge on the West Coast Main Line to the viaduct over the Solway Firth and into Cumbria. *Robert Leslie*

A Strathclyde PTE 'Sprinter' forms a Glasgow (Central)-Carlisle service on 21 June 1993. The bridge still stands in the background, but now carries a pipeline.

The town of **Dumfries** has seen no fewer than three stations, and while two quickly closed the third is still in use today.

The line linking Kilmarnock and Dumfries was completed in 1850 by the Glasgow & South Western Railway. With the line from Gretna Green having been opened as early as 1848, Dumfries quickly became established as an important junction as further lines sprouted from the town - to Castle Douglas in 1859, completed to Stranraer in 1861, and a further line to Lockerbie in 1863. The Cairn Valley Light Railway, linking Dumfries with Moniaive, opened in 1905, but traffic on this branch was always light and the line closed in 1943. With the closure of the 'Port Road' in 1965, all Stranraer traffic headed north via Mauchline.

The railway continues to serve Dumfries but it is a shadow of years gone by. Freight is minimal and 'Sprinters' form the passenger services to Glasgow, Ayr, Stranraer, Carlisle and Newcastle.

DUMFRIES GOODS YARD as it was on 27 April 1965. Standard 'Mogul' No 78051 is seen leaving the yard with a train of coal empties for the north. Note the well-populated sidings on the right and the coaling stage and edge of the turntable well on the left. *Douglas Hume*

On 23 July 1993 single-unit 'Sprinter' No 153361 is seen reversing into the up platform having travelled from the down platform and over the crossover. The coaling stage, turntable and depot have long since been demolished, but the sidings remain and are used by the Permanent Way Department. The main track formation is little altered - even the trap points under the first wagon of the goods train still exist.

DUMFRIES MPD (68B): Situated to the south of the station, the shed was similar in design to that at Ayr (67C). During its lifetime Dumfries boasted a reasonable allocation of mainly freight locos; in 1950 it had an allocation of almost 40 engines. The shed came into use in 1878, but with the closure of the 'Port Road' in June 1965 most of the workings disappeared and the shed duly closed in November 1966. The 'past' picture shows 'Black Five' No 45169 of 68B heading south with a parcels train for Carlisle on 13 June 1959. On shed is GNSR 4-4-0 No 49 *Gordon Highlander* being serviced during an SLS railtour (see page 13). *Robert Leslie*

Today's scene is a complete transformation - the shed has gone, replaced with the HQ of the Dumfries and Galloway Police. The buildings on the left survive intact, however, including the distinctive turret on the Station Hotel, top left in the trees. On 21 June 1993 'Sprinter' No 156433 arrives from Carlisle. Note that the foreground hut has gained a chimney pot.

DUMFRIES: A lengthy rail train rolls into Dumfries station on 13 June 1959 headed by 'WD' 2-8-0 No 90640. The station presents a very pleasing picture with its well-tended gardens in the left foreground. *Robert Leslie*

The station still has a neat and tidy appearance, although the centre road has been lifted, the footbridge has lost its roof, and the awning on the up platform has been shortened. However, the stonework has been cleaned, and it is heartening that most of the intricate ironwork survives. It is also interesting to note that the distinctive tall station lamps have been retained, as have the gardens; additional decorative woodwork adorns the gable end of the up platform buildings. On 22 June 1993 English Electric Class '37' No 37514 passes through with empty steel wagons from Stranraer.

DUMFRIES NORTH: On 7 July 1963 this was the view from the bridge north of the station looking south; the left-hand pair of lines are for Glasgow and the right-hand pair for Stranraer via the 'Port Road'. A Glasgow-bound parcels train makes a vigorous restart from the station behind 'Jubilee' No 45629 *Straits Settlements. Michael Mensing*

Thirty years later, on 22 June 1993, 'Sprinter' No 156442 heads for Glasgow (Central) . The photograph shows a much changed layout with the 'Port Road' gone but the Glasgow route using its alignment. The tower on the hill

has also gone and the land on the left is now a small industrial complex.

Crossing the road to take the 'going away shot', the photographer catches No 45629 heading smartly away towards Glasgow, the Stranraer line swinging away to the left. *Michael Mensing*

The 1993 shot shows again the change to the trackwork. The 'Port Road' is now just a long siding as far as Maxwelltown, and the Glasgow line regains its old course without the need for the reverse curves.

MONIAIVE: The railway came to Moniaive on 1 March 1905 by means of the Cairn Valley Light Railway, a 16-mile branch from Dumfries. The CVR was nominally independent, although it was in fact controlled by the G&SWR. A 'lock and block' system was used whereby the trains operated treadles on the single line to interact with the block instruments. The line closed to passengers on 3 May 1943, and completely in 1947; the station building is seen here in 1963. *Michael Mensing*

In the intervening 30 years there has been very little change apart from the large tree at the side and a further tree protruding from a chimney.

THORNHILL: A typical G&SWR scene from the '60s as Stanier '5MT' No 45028 drifts into Thornhill station with the 6.10 pm Carlisle-Glasgow (St Enoch) local on 25 July 1964. *Douglas Hume*

While the past picture is typical of its time, so is the present. The station is now closed and the platforms left to nature; the station house is now privately owned. The signal box, however, survives in use, as does the semaphore signalling. The fact that the station was a mile from the town may have hastened its demise.

CARRONBRIDGE (1): A Standard Class '5' 4-6-0 heads an up train over the viaduct to the south of Carronbridge station in 1963. The viaduct carries the railway over Carron Water and is 3 miles north of Thornhill. *Michael Mensing*
On 17 April 1993, some thirty years on, the tree growth has virtually obscured the view of the viaduct.

CARRONBRIDGE (2): Low evening sun highlights '5MT' No 44884 of Carlisle Kingmoor shed as it heads an up freight through Carronbridge station on 21 April 1965. *J. C. Beckett*

Twenty-eight years on and 'Sprinter' No 156506 heads south for Dumfries and Carlisle. The changes are quite dramatic: the pole route and the goods shed have gone and, in the case of the latter, a cottage has been revealed. The station building is now a private house which has lost its chimneys but gained two dormer windows.

DRUMLANRIG: Seen from above the northern portal of Drumlanrig Tunnel, a couple of miles north of Carronbridge, a 'Black Five' heads south with a train of empty 16-ton mineral wagons in 1963. Just look at the immaculate cutting sides! *Michael Mensing*

On 17 April 1993 a Strathclyde PTE Sprinter can barely be seen through the veritable forest of trees, and would be completely hidden from view in summer. No wonder the modern railway suffers from leaf-fall problems in the autumn.

ENTERKINFOOT: The 6.10 am Annan-Glasgow (St Enoch) is bathed in morning sunlight as it heads north over Enterkin Burn, just north of Drumlanrig, behind No 45463 on 9 June 1965. *J. C. Beckett*

On 15 June 1993 the viaduct is almost completely obscured by trees as a Carlisle-Glasgow 'Sprinter' heads north.

KIRKCONNEL station yard has altered little over the years. 'Jubilee' No 45621 *Northern Rhodesia* makes a rousing start from the station with the 10.50 am Dumfries-Glasgow (St Enoch) local on 9 September 1961. Note the coal bings (heaps) behind the locomotive. *Douglas Hume*

By 23 July 1993 the coal bings have all been removed as have the up siding and one of the down sidings. The station in the background remains, however, and is still open. The rather fine bracket signal is the main link between the views as Strathclyde PTE-liveried 'Sprinter' No 156506 accelerates the 09.19 service to Glasgow. While evidence of the coal industry has gone from the pictures, there is a new opencast mining development nearby.

NEW CUMNOCK: Looking west we see rebuilt 'Patriot' No 45512 *Bunsen* entering the station with the 12 noon Glasgow (St Enoch)-Carlisle stopping train on 9 September 1961. The 'Patriots' were rare on the G&SWR and no doubt Kingmoor had 'borrowed' the loco for a northbound train and this was the return working. Note the signal box at the end of the platform. *Douglas Hume*

New Cumnock station was re-opened to passengers on 29 May 1991 and this is commemorated by a stainless steel plaque in the station. The up platform has been shortened and the road bridge is used for passengers to cross the line by means of the new timber access steps. The signal box is still in use as are the semaphores, crossover and loops. The station is thus a pleasant blend of old and new.

AUCHINLECK as it appeared on 25 July 1964, with Stanier Class '5' No 45463 arriving with the 2.00 pm Glasgow (St Enoch)-Carlisle service. The railway came to Auchinleck from the Kilmarnock direction in August 1848 and was extended to New Cumnock in 1850. The station has a neat and tidy appearance and the gas lamps add character to the scene. *Douglas Hume*

Auchinleck station is one of several on the G&SWR line to be re-opened, and on a wet 31 July 1993 'Sprinter' No 156508 calls with the 11.03 Glasgow (Central)-Carlisle working. As can be seen there is very little of the original station left. The footbridge has been installed the opposite way round, the buildings are of the Strathclyde 'bus shelter' type (obscured by the bridge) and the lamps are now electric.

KILMARNOCK, HURLFORD MPD (67B): The town of Kilmarnock was served by Hurlford shed which was east of the town on the Strathaven line. It was a six-road shed and had an allocation of about 60 locomotives. It closed in December 1966. One of its Standard '4MT' 2-6-0s, No 76108, sits in the sun alongside the south wall of the shed building on 19 April 1965. *Noel A. Machell*

By way of comparison, a general view of the site today is offered showing the United Distillers development. The large, low building in the centre occupies roughly the same spot as the shed.

The first railway from the town of **Kilmarnock** was opened in 1812 with the line to Troon Harbour, and was operated by the Kilmarnock & Troon Railway Company. Kilmarnock was reached by a further line in 1843 with the opening of a line from Dalry. However, the townsfolk of Kilmarnock were rather put out that a town such as theirs was only served by a branch line.

The railway extended south to Auchinleck in 1848, on to Closeburn in October 1849 and by late 1850 the line was linked to Dumfries and the south. By June 1873 the railway was opened from Glasgow to Kilmarnock and named the Glasgow, Barrhead & Kilmarnock Joint Line. From the main line, branches were built to Galston in 1848 and Newmilns in 1850. With Kilmarnock sitting in the middle of the Ayrshire coalfield there was heavy coal traffic and this was reflected in the number of freight locomotives allocated to the local shed. At one time the shed at Hurlford had an allocation of 100 locomotives. There was also a locomotive works, opened in 1856, situated at the north end of the station in a triangle, one side of which was the line to Troon and the other the line to Dalry.

The bulk of the Ayrshire branch lines closed to passenger traffic in the 1960s and with the closure of many of the collieries much of the goods traffic ceased, never to be replaced.

Nowadays Kilmarnock enjoys a fairly frequent service to Glasgow and a less frequent service to the south, ie Dumfries and Carlisle. There are also a few trains to Ayr and Stranraer, but unfortunately very little freight.

The railway workshops of Andrew Barclay & Co remain in the town, but apart from the occasional steam special the station now sees only 'Sprinters'.

Below 'Royal Scot' 4-6-0 No 46113 *Cameronian* passes Kilmarnock East Junction, on its approach to the station, with the 3.50 pm Glasgow (St Enoch)-Dumfries on 29 June 1957. The lines to the left lead to Barassie and Ayr, the ones in the centre to Dalry and Irvine. *Brian Morrison*

Right KILMARNOCK: 'Royal Scot' No 46108 *Seaforth Highlander* pulls away with the heavy 10.35 am Leeds-Glasgow (St Enoch) service on 29 June 1967. To the right of the gantry of semaphores are two local trains in the bay platforms, bound for Darvel and Ayr respectively; both have '2P' power in the shape of 4-4-0s Nos 40612 and 40610. *Brian Morrison*

The same location on 17 June 1993 shows 'Sprinter' No 156432 on the 16.34 to Glasgow (Central). The buildings on the up side have all gone, but the large Johnny Walker building on the extreme left still stands. The station building on the down side has been declared unsafe and may need to be partly demolished; the glass has been removed from part of the awnings. Semaphore signals have been replaced by colour lights. Platform 1, from where the picture was taken, was not in use at the time of the visit.

61

LUGTON: Standard Class '3' 2-6-0 No 77019 of Hurlford shed (67B) trundles through Lugton station with a south-bound freight on 15 September 1962, while a Bristol/ECW railbus waits at the down signal. *Douglas Hume*

The station at Lugton has long gone, as have the platforms. However, it retains a signal box and a fine selection of semaphore signals. The apparent double track is not what it seems - it is in fact two single lines, the nearer one being the Giffen branch (see pages 113-14) and the far line the G&SWR route to Carlisle. 'Sprinter' No 156507 forms a Glasgow (Central)-Kilmarnock service on 24 July 1993.

CALDWELL station was the setting chosen by the BBC film unit to film scenes for *Dr Finlay's Casebook*. On 11 October 1966 smartly turned out 'J36' 0-6-0 No 65345 was provided along with two Caledonian coaches and they are seen here entering 'Tannochbrae', which has been dressed with period detail for the occasion. *Douglas Hume*

Caldwell station is no more but the station house now forms a modernised private house and is seen on 24 July 1993 with 'Sprinter' No 156430 passing on a Glasgow service. As the station footbridge, from which the original picture was obtained, has gone, the present picture was obtained by use of a telephoto lens from the road bridge to the east.

BARRHEAD: An interesting view of Barrhead station at lunchtime on 23 December 1961 with McIntosh '652' Class 0-6-0 No 57643 running through the station on its way back to its home shed at Hurlford. In the bay platform stands Fairburn 2-6-4T No 42193 with the 1.37 pm train to Glasgow (St Enoch). *Douglas Hume*

On 24 July 1993 'Sprinter' No 156434 runs into the bay with a working from Glasgow (Central). The water tank on the right has been removed, as have the semaphores; the signal box remains but is out of use. The large factory building on the left has been re-roofed and has lost its ventilators.

KENNISHEAD: 'Super power' for the 12.23 pm Glasgow (St Enoch)-Kilmarnock local on 23 December 1961 as Class '5' No 45192 and Standard 2-6-0 No 77016 roll into Kennishead station, between Pollockshaws and Nitshill on the Kilmarnock line. *Douglas Hume*

The station today is dominated by blocks of high-rise flats that tower over the railway. The station buildings have all gone, as has the bracket signal. 'Sprinter' No 156433 calls at the station on 24 July 1993 with a train for Barrhead.

CROSSMYLOOF was well known, not for its station, but for its ice-rink, which is the large building on the left of the picture as '2P' No 40608 arrives with the 6.11 pm Glasgow (St Enoch)-Kilmarnock train on 20 August 1959. *Douglas Hume*

By 24 July 1993 the ice-rink has been demolished and replaced by a Safeway supermarket, and this building dominates the scene as 'Sprinter' No 156431 arrives with the 15.18 to East Kilbride.

STRATHBUNGO: Standard '4MT' 2-6-4T No 80130 rolls into Strathbungo station with the 5.33 pm Glasgow (St Enoch)-East Kilbride train on 24 May 1962. The junction beyond the bridge, Muirhouse South Junction, is where the lines from Glasgow (Central), on the left, meet the lines from Larkfield Junction which was the route from St Enoch. *Douglas Hume*

The station has now gone, but the booking hall on the bridge survives as shops. As the platforms have been removed, the picture was taken from an existing footbridge across the railway.

The 'Port Road' and branches

The line from Dumfries westwards to Stranraer passed through bleak moorland and over several rivers which required major bridge and viaduct construction. While the railway passed through several towns such as Dalbeattie, Castle Douglas and Newton Stewart, the great attraction was Ireland, and initially the railway strived to reach Portpatrick on the coast.

The first step to Portpatrick from Dumfries took place on 7 November 1859 with the opening of the Castle Douglas & Dumfries Railway. From Castle Douglas the line was extended to Stranraer on 12 March 1861 and to Portpatrick on 28 August 1862. A branch then had to be built down the steep incline to the harbour, and this opened on 1 October 1862.

Meanwhile, a line to Wigtown and Whithorn was opened from Newton Stewart on 9 July 1877, and from this line at Millisle, a short branch to Garlieston on the coast. The Portpatrick Railway was soon in financial trouble, as was the Wigtown Railway, and the two merged in 1885. The other major branch off the main line was from Castle Douglas to Kirkcudbright, which opened for traffic on 17 February 1864. The line from Stranraer to Portpatrick became a branch line and the lucrative Irish traffic was concentrated on Stranraer.

The 'Port Road' closed on 14 June 1965. Stranraer remains a busy port to this day, but the vast bulk of goods now goes by road, an all too familiar story.

Left LONGWOOD BANK was three and a half miles from Dumfries. Standard Class '4' No 76072 crosses the viaduct on the 1 in 73 incline with the 8.07 am Dumfries-Kirkcudbright local on 22 April 1965. Dumfries acquired two of these Standard '4s' in the 1960s and they were put to good use on the Kirkcudbright trains. No 76073 was the other loco. and it worked the final Kirkcudbright train on 1 May 1965. *J. C. Beckett*

The present-day view on 22 February 1993 for once shows fewer trees than the earlier shot. The viaduct still stands; the large building on the right is Goldilea Private Nursing Home.

LOCHANHEAD: On 13 June 1959 'Jubilee' 4-6-0 No 45731 *Perseverance* storms through the cutting at the head of the 12.20 pm (SO) Newcastle-Stranraer train. This locomotive was allocated to Carlisle Kingmoor shed for many years and was no stranger to the 'Port Road'. *Robert Leslie*

A visit to this location on 16 April 1993 showed the cutting sides over-run with trees and shrubs. The picture was taken to the left of the original viewpoint because of the bushes that have grown up in the intervening years. Note the overhead power line which follows the trackbed and which is seen in some of the following pictures.

KIRKGUNZEON: The undulating countryside, so typical of south-west Scotland, is much in evidence as Fairburn 2-6-4T No 42689 heads a freight towards Dumfries on 8 July 1963. *Michael Mensing*

Once again the modern scene shows little trace of what was once a main-line railway. The view on 22 February 1993 shows the station house remaining in the background, now privately owned. The power lines define the former route, but all other traces of the railway have been erased from the scene.

SOUTHWICK in 1963, and Standard 2-6-4T No 80023 arrives with a train for Dumfries. Note the superb gas lamp, footbridge and signal box on the left of the picture. *Michael Mensing*

There is no visual evidence of the former station at all, but detailed inspection of the site revealed remains of the platform edgings hidden in the undergrowth. Part of the trackbed has been infilled to provide an access road for Forestry Commission vehicles. The power lines still follow the trackbed.

APPROACHING URR BRIDGE: Another picture of the 8.07 am Dumfries-Kirkcudbright train on 22 April 1965 behind Standard 2-6-0 No 76072. The train is approaching the bridge over Urr Water, between Dalbeattie and Castle Douglas, just a few weeks before the closure of the line. *J. C. Beckett*

On 22 February 1993 it is a familiar sight - the trackbed is disused and has piles of rubble on it, the background forest has been extended and the tree on the right has reached maturity.

URR BRIDGE: The metal bridge spanning Urr Water was one of many picturesque locations on this line. On 21 April 1965 a Stanier 'Black Five' and a Standard 2-6-0 head the combined Stranraer and Kirkcudbright trains across the bridge; the train will split at Castle Douglas. The Urr was one of seven major rivers crossed between Dumfries and Stranraer. *J. C. Beckett*

By 22 February 1993 very little has changed apart from the removal of the track and the bridge.

CASTLE DOUGLAS (1): Class '2P' 4-4-0 No 40623 stands in Castle Douglas station on 1 July 1961 with a local train for Dumfries. The service between Castle Douglas and Dumfries ceased when the route closed on 14 June 1965. *Gavin W. Morrison*

On 16 April 1993 all trace of the station has been swept away and the site is now an industrial estate; this picture was taken in the Local Authority Depot. The linking features are the background trees on the right and the distant building with the distinctive chimneys.

CASTLE DOUGLAS (2): The town of Castle Douglas is in the background as Standard tank No 80023 approaches with the 9.30 am train from Kirkcudbright on 18 July 1963. The branch closed with the rest of the 'Port Road' main line on 14 June 1965. *Michael Mensing*

Apart from the removal of the railway and the church spire, there was little visual change on 22 February 1993.

BRIDGE OF DEE: Moving further down the Kirkcudbright branch we see a Fairburn 2-6-4T passing the site of Bridge of Dee station in 1963. The branch was normally the preserve of Standard '4s' Nos 76072/3. *Michael Mensing*
    A visit on 22 February 1993 found that the station house is now a private dwelling and the trackbed and station area are being developed as a very attractive garden. The goods platform still remains behind the small fir trees.

TARFF: Standard '4MT' tank No 80023 of Dumfries shed approaches Tarff station with a railtour on 15 April 1963. Judging by the leading coach it was not well patronised and there is an absence of heads out of the windows. *Rodney Lissenden*

Nearly 30 years on and what a mess! The cottage behind the loco has gone and the embankment is now covered in bushes and trees. A large corrugated-iron-clad building has been erected on the site of the goods yard, but the station building survives, as does a short length of platform. Generally, though, the scene is fairly depressing.

KIRKCUDBRIGHT: The Kirkcudbright Railway opened in February 1864 and services lasted just over one hundred years. Here is the station on 24 April 1965, just days before closure; Standard Class '4MT' 2-6-4T No 80117 stands with the 4.51 pm to Dumfries. Just out of the picture to the left stood the single-road engine shed, which closed in 1955. A unique feature of the shed was the engine cleaner's house adjoining the rear of the building. *Fred Landery*

The sole remaining feature of the area is the church and spire. No trace of the railway exists, and the whole station site is now a housing development.

LOCH KEN VIADUCT: Fairburn 2-6-4T No 42689 approaches the bridge over the middle of Loch Ken, 7 miles north-west of Castle Douglas, with the 3.50 pm from Stranraer (Town) to Dumfries on 19 July 1963. Note that from Castle Douglas the 'Port Road' was single line until it met the route from Girvan at Challoch Junction near Stranraer, a distance of 48 miles. *Michael Mensing*

On 16 April 1993 the viewpoint had to be nearer the bridge as vegetation obscured the exact position. The trackbed is now used as a farm track and, despite a notice warning that the bridge is unsafe, there were lots of wheeltracks across it! Loch Ken is a very tranquil location and is used extensively by yachting enthusiasts.

BIG WATER OF FLEET VIADUCT, as its name implies, spans the valley of the Big Water of Fleet; Gatehouse station was 2 miles to the west, and the town of Gatehouse of Fleet 6 miles to the south. The viaduct was the largest structure on the line, and is seen here from the south-west on 1 July 1961 as Class '5' 4-6-0 No 44885 crosses with a Dumfries-Stranraer local train. Note the photographer's motorcycle on the left. *Gavin W. Morrison*

As can be seen from the picture taken on a wet 16 April 1993, the viaduct remains as a silent memorial to the 'Port Road'. It is completely intact and is a great compliment to the gangs of men involved in its construction in the mid-1800s.

CREETOWN (SPITTAL LENNIES): 'Crab' 2-6-0 No 42919 pauses at Creetown station with a down pick-up freight on 15 July 1963. The loco is pulling forward to take water before heading for Stranraer. No 42919 was a Dumfries (68B) loco, spending many years at that shed. *Michael Mensing*

Nearly 30 years later, while the track, signal box and pole route have gone, the buildings still remain. The main station building is in a very poor condition, the concrete-roofed building has fared better, while the large goods shed is receiving attention to the roof. The trackbed is deep in stagnant water, making access to the up platform impossible. The picture was obtained by going as far left as possible and holding the camera high on a monopod. Some connection with the steam age is retained as the yard is used by a coal merchant.

NEWTON STEWART: The railway came to Newton Stewart in 1861 when the Portpatrick Railway opened from Castle Douglas to Stranraer; the line was extended to Portpatrick the following year. The view on 19 July 1963 shows Stanier '5MT' No 45485 of Stranraer shed working the 1.40 pm Stranraer (Harbour)-Dumfries service. *Michael Mensing*

The same spot on 14 June 1993 shows that all evidence of the station has been removed, the site now being occupied by a Royal Mail sorting office. The tall trees are the only linking feature.

NEWTON STEWART JUNCTION: To the west of the station Standard '4MT' 2-6-0 No 76073 approaches from the Stranraer direction with a mixed freight in 1963. The Whithorn branch swung away on the extreme right of the picture with the junction in front of the signal box; the branch home signal can be seen immediately above the loco cab roof. The station was beyond the background bridge and the turntable and the engine shed out of the picture on the right. *Michael Mensing*

Thirty years later the road bridge has been demolished and the road realigned to the west. As a result, an exactly duplicated viewpoint could not be obtained. Industrial units now occupy the trackbed and goods yard. The corner of the building with the curved roof is sinking as it stands over the old turntable pit. The brick building to the extreme right is the old two-road engine shed, which was closed in 1959 having opened in 1895. The structure is not the original building, as the earlier shed had been reduced to a ruin in 1920 with the present building erected the following year.

WIGTOWN: This was the first station down the Whithorn branch, and Caley 0-6-0 No 57375, for many years the regular branch engine, stands in the station on 4 September 1961 with a Newton Stewart-Whithorn goods train. The branch opened on 9 July 1877 and closed on 5 October 1964. *Douglas Hume*

By 23 July 1993 the railway has gone completely. A part of the platform remains on the left and the bridge still exists at the end of the overgrown cutting. The houses on the left and roadway on the right confirm the location.

SORBIE: No 57375 stands with the branch goods on 4 September 1961 alongside the creamery. *Douglas Hume*

The scene is now transformed and it took the photographer some while to work out the changes. The old creamery had been demolished and a new one built 100 yards further south; the new creamery is now also closed. The road bridge has been demolished and the road re-aligned to run across the south of the station. Careful study identifies the approach to the old road bridge in the background, the bridge itself being behind the new garage. The old building on the platform can now be seen behind the bush as part of a beautifully restored and privately owned station house.

MILLISLE JUNCTION: The branch from here to Garlieston closed to passengers as far back as 1 March 1903, having opened in 1877, although it remained open for freight until October 1964. On 15 April 1963 Caley No 57375 takes a railtour down the branch, and looking at the stock it is as well that it was a fine day! It is doubtful if the Health and Safety Executive would permit it today! The line to Whithorn runs past the far side of the fine signal box. *Rodney Lissenden*

A herd of cows are the occupants of the site on 14 June 1993 as the trackbed is returned to agriculture. There was a station building and platform to the left of the pictures, and this is now a private house. There was no platform on the Garlieston branch.

GARLIESTON station was at the end of the mile-long spur from Millisle Junction, and the line stopped just short of Garlieston Harbour. No 57375 is seen again on the branch goods on 4 September 1961. Built in 1883, this Drummond 'Standard Goods' worked for many years in the area. *Douglas Hume*

A part of the platform remains hidden by the bush in the centre of the picture. Exactly the same viewpoint would have produced a picture of the bush, so a compromise position was used which shows the roofs of the houses on the right and the large tree on the left which was just to the left of the engine in the 'past' picture. The goods yard is now a private site for trailer caravans, as seen here on a wet day in July 1993.

WHITHORN stood at the end of the branch from Newton Stewart, and again No 57375 is seen on 4 September 1961 running round its train. *Douglas Hume*

The present picture reveals no trace of the railway. The view on 23 July 1993 shows that the former goods yard is being used as the site of a new Fire Station which was in course of construction. The large house on the left and the house in the centre background tie the past and present together. The station was at the north end of this attractive town.

GLENLUCE: Back on the 'Port Road', the 8.57 am Castle Douglas-Stranraer Town passenger train is seen just after leaving Glenluce station, in the charge of Stanier '5MT' No 45432 on 12 July 1963. The train will shortly cross the viaduct which dominates the western approach to the town and is still standing today. *Michael Mensing*

By 14 June 1993 the railway has gone and the trackbed has been left to nature. The local graveyard, just visible on the extreme right, still remains and is kept in good order. The drystone wall in the field on the left has been replaced by a hedge.

STRANRAER HARBOUR (I): A housing estate forms the backdrop as Class '5MT' No 45061 makes its approach to the harbour with the 12.01pm local train from Dumfries on 12 July 1963. Even though it is high summer the cutting sides are neat and tidy. *Michael Mensing*

By 15 June 1993 there has been little change to the background apart from some replacement windows and the reduced number of television aerials - cable TV perhaps? On the railway the cutting now has much undergrowth, the pole route has gone and 'Sprinters' have replaced loco-hauled passenger trains. Here No 156439 forms the 08.23 from Glasgow (Central).

The railway arrived in **Stranraer** on 12 March 1861 with the completion of the line from Dumfries and Castle Douglas. This line was known as the Portpatrick Railway and the line was extended to Portpatrick itself on 28 August 1862. This proved to be a costly blunder as the stretch from Stranraer to Portpatrick included a 1 in 57 gradient and with the harbour at Portpatrick being situated well below rail level, the final yards to the harbour were down a 1 in 35 gradient. It was in 1874 that the authorities decided to concentrate on Stranraer, and the Portpatrick line was relegated to branch status.

Three years later, in 1877, the line from Girvan reached Stranraer and with it the long-awaited connection to the west of Scotland.

The Portpatrick branch closed on 6 February 1950 and with the closure of the line from Dumfries to Challoch (Dunragit) Junction on 14 June 1965 the 'Port Road' was no more, and all trains from the south for Stranraer Harbour were re-routed via Mauchline.

Stranraer remains a thriving port to this day but, sadly, nearly all the freight traffic to and from Ireland comes by road. In 1993 there was only a thrice weekly freight train of export steel from the south to Stranraer.

STRANRAER HARBOUR (2): Crossing the road, No 45061 runs the final yards into the Harbour station on 12 July 1963. *Michael Mensing*

On 14 June 1993 'Sprinter' No 156501 departs with the 21.14 to Glasgow (Central). The track layout has been rationalised, with the old goods yard now part of the checking and parking areas for lorries and trailers awaiting the ferry to Larne in Northern Ireland. Only one, seldom used, siding remains. This typifies the growth in road transport over the last 30 years and the decline of freight carried by rail. In the distance the signal gantry at the approach to the station survives, as does the signal box. The ferry in the present picture is the Stena Sealink vessel *Stena Galloway*. The sun is still high in the sky at these latitudes in the middle of June.

STRANRAER TOWN (1): Stanier 4-6-0 No 45432 runs round its train at Town station in 1963. *Michael Mensing*

Town station closed to passengers on 7 March 1966. On 15 June 1993 Class '37' No 37718 can be seen in the distance waiting to depart with a train of empty steel wagons for Tees-side. At that time the train ran three times a week on Tuesdays, Thursdays and Saturdays, and was the only freight traffic to Stranraer by rail. The station is not in public use but the buildings are used by British Rail Engineers. The line used to continue beyond the buffer stops for a further five miles to Portpatrick. The old MPD building can still be seen beyond the station.

STRANRAER TOWN (2): Looking west this time at the other end of the station, we see ex-LMS Compound 4-4-0 No 40920 pulling away with the morning train to Glasgow (St Enoch) on 3 August 1956. This loco was shedded at Ayr (67C) for many years but it survived for less than three years from the date of this picture. *David A. Anderson*

The station still survives as a Civil Engineers' Depot, and the platform end can still be seen above the point lever on 23 July 1993.

STRANRAER MPD (68C) was made up of four main buildings, the Joint Shed, the Girvan Shed, the Erecting Shop (which was the original Portpatrick Works) and the Caledonian Shed. The shed only ever had a small allocation of locos at any one time, about a dozen, but it played host to many visiting engines working in from Carlisle and Glasgow. Latterly it was coded 67F, and closed in October 1966 with its last loco, a Stanier 'Black Five', being transferred to Ayr MPD (67C). This view of the Joint Shed on 7 September 1964 shows no fewer than five 4-6-0s on shed: three Stanier 'Black Fives', a Standard Class '5MT' and a 'Jubilee', No 45742 *Connaught*. *Hugh Ballantyne*

Today finds the main shed building still standing, but it presents a rather untidy appearance as part of King Bros Scrap Merchants. The extensive sidings adjacent to the shed are still in situ, but did not appear to have had much use when visited on 15 June 1993.

Past and Present Colour

South West Scotland

CRAIGENHILL: On 21 September 1963 two Clayton diesels, Nos D8522 and D8546, approach Craigenhill Junction with an up freight. This junction was situated halfway between Carluke and Lanark Junction, and the short branch served a lime mine.

The 'present' picture, taken on 1 November 1994, shows that the signal box has long gone, and the tree growth has hidden any sign of the branch trackbed. A railway telecommunications tower has been erected on the down side. *W. A. C. Smith/Keith Sanders*

BEITH: On 15 September 1962 one of the two Bristol/ECW railbuses stands in the Caledonian and Glasgow & South Western joint station at Beith. This was the terminus of the short branch from Lugton.

The scene on 17 September 1994 is much changed, as the whole station site is now a housing estate. Careful investigation does, however, reveal the ornate chimneys of a house in the background of both pictures. *Douglas Hume/Keith Sanders*

MONTGREENAN: On 21 July 1973, because of engineering works in the Glasgow area, which prevented direct access from Glasgow Central to the West Coast Main Line or to the Kilmarnock line, trains were diverted via Paisley and Dalry in order to reach Kilmarnock and the Sou'West line. English Electric Type 4 No D412 is seen passing the site of Montgreenan station with the 14.05 Glasgow Central-London Euston service.

On 1 November 1994 the trackbed is clearly visible, and behind the trees the station building is still standing and in use as a private residence. *Douglas Hume/Keith Sanders*

PORT GLASGOW: Stanier 'Black Five' No 45360 calls at the station in early 1962. This picture was taken from a foot-bridge that ran across the west end of the station.

The footbridge no longer exists, nor does the bay platform, so a slightly different position had to be adopted for this view of unit No 303087 departing for Gourock on 1 November 1994. On the hillside one block of flats has been demolished, but otherwise there has been little change to the surrounding buildings. The red board on the plat-form is the back of a large mirror so that the driver can see down the train for 'driver only operation'. *W. A. C. Smith/Keith Sanders*

PAISLEY GILMOUR STREET: Fairburn 2-6-4T No 42264 restarts the 3.15 pm Glasgow Central-Wemyss Bay service from Gilmour Street on 29 September 1962. The grimy condition of the locomotive and station was so typical of the time.

By comparison, the present-day scene is quite colourful, with unit No 316267 departing for Gourock on 1 November 1994. The station has received new awnings, and even boasts plants around the bases of the lighting poles. *W. A. C. Smith/Keith Sanders*

PAISLEY ST JAMES: The 'Jones Goods', Highland Railway 4-6-0 No 103, is seen in charge of one of the famous 'Easter Rambler' tours on 17 April 1965 while covering the Renfrewshire lines.

Today the station is unstaffed, and accommodation for passengers is provided by a small 'bus shelter' on each platform. On 1 November 1994 unit No 318265 heads for Glasgow Central. Many buildings in the area have been demolished, which adds to the feeling of dereliction. *Douglas Hume/Keith Sanders*

MAXWELL PARK: BR Standard 2-6-4T No 80002 accelerates the 6.12 pm Glasgow Central-Cathcart 'Inner Circle' train away from Maxwell Park station on 12 April 1962. Upon withdrawal from active service, this locomotive was used as a stationary boiler at Cowlairs Carriage Depot. From there it was saved from being cut up and is now at the Keighley & Worth Valley Railway awaiting restoration.

On a rather dull 2 November 1994, electric unit No 303040 gets under way in virtually the same surroundings. The absence of the white building on the right-hand side is the major change. *W. A. C. Smith/Keith Sanders*

IBROX EAST JUNCTION: BR Standard Class '4' 'Mogul' No 76001 works a freight train off the Govan branch at Ibrox East Junction on 29 September 1962.

Thirty-two years on, only the gas-holder and the low retaining wall remain from the 'past' picture. Ibrox station closed on 6 February 1967, and the present-day simplified layout of just two lines came with the electrification of the line. Unit No 303034 heads for Glasgow Central on 1 November 1994. *W. A. C. Smith/Keith Sanders*

Ayrshire lines

GIRVAN: The railway came to Girvan on 24 May 1860 with the opening of the Maybole & Girvan Railway, and the line was extended south on 5 October 1877. The Girvan & Portpatrick Railway, as it was known, connected Girvan with Challoch (Dunragit) Junction and thus access to Portpatrick. In 1905 a coastal route from Girvan to Ayr was opened, thus bringing the railway to several small villages on the coast; this was known as the 'Maidens line'. The line was poorly patronised and the northern stretch from Maidens to Alloway Junction, south of Ayr, finally closed on 31 May 1933. The southern section from Maidens to Girvan remained open until March 1942, and served the prestigious Turnberry Hotel. After the war the section from Alloway Junction to Heads of Ayr was re-opened for traffic to and from Butlin's Holiday Camp; this lasted until 12 September 1968. This 1973 view of Girvan station is looking north as a three-car DMU arrives with a Stranraer service. *Michael Mensing*

On 15 June 1993 a Class '156' 'Sprinter' in Strathclyde PTE livery arrives with the 12.43 to Stranraer. In the opposite direction, unseen Class '37' No 37718 takes a train of empty steel wagons north on to the single track. The buildings on the southbound platform have been completely removed and replaced with ornamental wrought ironwork; the subway canopies are also a thing of the past, but the signal box, semaphores and northbound platform buildings remain.

DAILY: 'Black Five' No 44795 arrives with the 6.20 pm Girvan-Glasgow (St Enoch) train on 8 August 1959; note the Caledonian route indicator on the centre lamp bracket. *W. A. C. Smith*

Thirty-three years on, not only have the platforms gone but the line has been singled. The station building on the left is still standing but in a poor condition. Foliage all but obliterates the view, but the tree behind the station retains its very distinctive shape. The station yard is now used by the local coal merchant.

KILKERRAN: Two three-car 'Cross-country' units roll into Kilkerran station in 1973 with a Stranraer service. Kilkerran was the next station north of Dailly and had a level crossing at the north end, the gates of which are hidden between the bushes and signal box. *Michael Mensing*

On 15 June 1993 'Sprinter' No 156433 heads for Stranraer in dull weather. The line is singled but the signal box remains to operate the lifting barriers, which have replaced the traditional gates, and to control the passing loop beyond the crossing. The station house is now in private ownership and the bushes have grown.

The railway reached the town of **Ayr** as early as 1839 with the opening of the line from Ayr to Irvine by the Glasgow, Paisley, Kilmarnock & Ayr Railway Company. The line from Ayr to Glasgow was open throughout the following year.

The Ayr & Dalmellington Railway opened in 1856 and the Ayr & Maybole Railway came into being a year later. The route from Ayr to Mauchline opened in September 1870 and the Ayr to Stranraer line on 5 October 1877. A light railway was opened in 1905 serving the villages along the coast between Ayr and Girvan, principally Turnberry with its golf course and hotel.

The Ayr to Dalmellington line closed in April 1964 and the Alloway to Heads of Ayr line closed four year later.

Ayr today is still an important railway centre with the lines to Stranraer, Glasgow and Kilmarnock still open to passenger traffic. Much of the coal traffic has vanished, but a small amount remains. However, with the line to Glasgow now electrified, the railway's future at Ayr seems assured for many years to come.

AYR: Standard Class '4' 2-6-0 No 76098 pulls out of the station with a holiday extra bound for Aberdeen on 17 July 1965. *S. C. Nash*
The scene on 17 June 1993 is not vastly different apart from the overhead wires, motive power and modern signs. The mass of the Station Hotel remains as a backdrop as EMU No 318266 departs with the 14.15 to Glasgow (Central).

101

AYR MPD (67C): This 1 September 1957 picture shows two Class '08' diesel shunters with Stanier '5MT' No 45121 and Standard '4MT' 2-6-4Ts Nos 80030 and 80009 in front of the distinctive building. This six-road shed was situated between Ayr and Newton on Ayr, within a triangle of lines and adjacent to Ayr United Football Club. The shed had a substantial allocation of motive power, both passenger and goods, the latter for working the considerable coal traffic of the Ayrshire coalfields. The shed closed as a steam depot in December 1966 when the last two locos, Nos 76096 and 76101, were withdrawn. *Gavin W. Morrison*

The site is now occupied by a more modern building with roller-shutter doors displaying the Railfreight Coal subsector symbols. On 17 June 1993 Class '56' No 56123 *Drax Power Station* stands alongside the maintenance shed.

ANNBANK JUNCTION: A busy time on 24 June 1966 as 'Black Five' No 45167 with a train of empty 16-ton mineral wagons takes the branch to Drongan and Killoch while sister loco No 44989 waits to come off the line from Mauchline Junction. *Roger Siviter*

The view in June 1993 shows that both routes have been singled and the bing (coal heap) in the background has shrunk dramatically. The steps on the left-hand side have gone, as has the signal box to which they led. The background houses remain unaltered, however, apart from various garden sheds and garages.

DALMELLINGTON was at the end of the Waterside branch from Holehouse Junction, and provides a classic scene of a small Scottish station with the church spire in the background. Class '2P' 4-4-0 No 40590 of Ayr shed stands with the 5.30 pm to Ayr on 5 March 1955. Passenger services were withdrawn on 6 April 1964. *W. A. C. Smith*

The site of the station on 15 June 1993 shows a complete transformation; only the church and the adjacent building identify it as the same place. The railway has been erased from the landscape and the site occupied by a light industrial unit. Behind the photographer a large school, Doon Academy, now stands astride the trackbed.

MUIRKIRK (1): A Metro-Cammell two-car DMU sits in Muirkirk station to form the 12.41 pm to Lanark on 12 June 1964. This service lasted but a few months more, the last passenger train to Lanark running in October of the same year. The Muirkirk to Auchinleck passenger service had ceased even earlier, in July 1950. *Fred Landery*

The station, signal box and track have all gone, and the trackbed between the platform faces has been infilled. The only railway-related feature is the station house (hidden behind the DMU in the 'past' picture) which is now privately owned. The station was a good half mile from the town centre.

MUIRKIRK (2): A view of the signal box on the platform with Caledonian McIntosh '812' Class 0-6-0 No 57566 of Ardrossan shed (67D) standing in the platforms on 30 June 1963. Although Muirkirk was a G&SWR station, the route on to Lanark was Caledonian. *Rodney Lissenden*

The scene looking east in June 1993 shows a complete absence of railway-related items. While the land is now lying derelict there was evidence of the site having been used by road transport, as a loading ramp had been built and the remains of a weighbridge were found.

MUIRKIRK MPD: No 57566 again, standing on shed on 30 June 1963. Muirkirk, a sub-shed to Hurlford (67B), had at one time an allocation of 12 locomotives, but with the closure of the Lugar Ironworks in 1923 a decline in the shed's fortunes set in. The shed was rebuilt as late as 1950 and reduced from a four-road building to one containing two roads. The shed closed in October 1964 with its remaining workings taken over by Hurlford. *Rodney Lissenden*

A visit on 17 June 1993 found all trace of the railway gone and in its place a go-kart track. Still evident is the clock tower of the Community Centre, under its new title of the Strathclyde Adult Education Centre.

BARASSIE: A six-car DMU pauses at the station with a Glasgow (St Enoch)-Ayr service in July 1961. A feature of the station was the well-maintained gardens and the generally neat and well-kept appearance of the station buildings. The lines to the right lead to Kilmarnock. *David A. Anderson*

Looking at the scene on 17 June 1993, the line to Kilmarnock has been singled and slewed away from the platform face. The station buildings have gone along with the flower beds and the station is unstaffed. The main Glasgow-Ayr line is now electrified and a Class '318' EMU forms the 15.06 to Ayr. The prominent building in the middle of the picture is the local golf clubhouse, and the course is used for qualifying rounds when the British Open Golf Championship is held at Royal Troon. Behind the photographer is the Barassie Overhead Line Depot and a run-round loop, the latter often used by the Irvine-Burngullow (Cornwall) china clay train.

DRYBRIDGE is approximately half way between Barassie and Kilmarnock and here we see '2P' 4-4-0 No 40695 working the 5.10 pm Ayr-Kilmarnock train on 25 June 1960. It is interesting to note that this train merited a rake of eight coaches, but there seem to be no patrons on the platform. *W. A. C. Smith*

The picture taken on 17 June 1993 shows 'Sprinter' No 156434 going away from the camera with a Newcastle-Stranraer service. As has already been seen opposite, the line is now singled and is aligned away from the surviving platform face. The buildings on the south side have gone together with the north-side platform awning, while the original station building has had some additions in its current role as a private house.

ARDROSSAN, SOUTH BEACH: Standard 2-6-4T No 80035 arrives with the 3.56 pm Glasgow (St Enoch)-Largs train on 29 June 1959. *W. A. C. Smith*

On 17 June 1993 EMU No 318262 leaves for Ardrossan Town station. The line is now electrified and there is only one platform face, the line being bi-directional. (It is thought that the line on the left was also bi-directional, and carried the Hunterston-Ravenscraig iron ore trains prior to the closure of Ravenscraig Steelworks.) The up platform has been removed and the original station buildings on the down side have been replaced by one of ultra-modern design. In the background the church tower survives, as does the school building on the right. A large tower block of flats now dominates the scene.

ARDROSSAN, HOLM JUNCTION: Immediately to the west of South Beach station is Holm Junction, and this 1962 view shows a Park Royal railbus on an Ardrossan Town-Kilmarnock service coming off the branch from the left which leads to Ardrossan Town station and Winton Pier; the lines to the right lead to West Kilbride and Largs. Between the two routes can be seen Ardrossan shed (67D). At one time the shed boasted an allocation of over 40 locos, mostly for local passenger and goods traffic. The shed closed in February 1965. *W. L. Callan*

The present picture shows EMU No 318251 approaching with an Ardrossan Town-Glasgow (Central) working. Holm Junction formed the eastern junction of a triangle. The left spur went to Castlemill Junction then continued to the Town station, while the right spur went to Parkhouse Junction and then on to Largs. The chord between Castlemill Junction and Parkhouse Junction no longer exists.

LARGS: A general view of Largs station on 12 September 1959 shows a busy railway scene. 'Jubilee' 4-6-0 No 45731 *Perseverance* departs with the 4.00 pm to Glasgow (St Enoch) while LMS '2P' 4-4-0 No 40625 waits in the platform on the left. Largs was a bustling coastal resort helped in no small way by the coming of the railway in June 1885. The station had many platforms with associated sidings and during the summer saw a great deal of excursion traffic. *S. C. Nash*

The station is now a two-platform terminus at the end of what is no more than a long siding from Holm Junction, served by Class '318' EMUs on an hourly service. This presumably is a reflection of the much reduced rail traffic from city to seaside at holiday times, most of it now going by road. No 318257 is seen arriving with a train from Glasgow on 18 June 1993. The church spire in the background survives, but the large building behind the house on the right has gone. The east side of the old station is now a bus and coach service depot; however, the remains of the long platform can still be seen.

Renfrewshire lines

BARRMILL: A branch to Beith left the G&SWR Glasgow (St Enoch)-Kilmarnock line at Lugton Junction, and Barrmill was the only intermediate station (the G&SWR Glasgow-Kilmarnock line, including the Beith branch, was in fact a joint G&SWR/Caledonian operation). In the background, to the east of the station, was Barrmill Junction from where a line ran to Giffen to join up with the Caley line from Glasgow to Ardrossan. The Lanarkshire & Ayrshire Railway from Barrmill to Ardrossan opened on 4 September 1888, and the Beith Town to Barrmill section closed on 5 October 1964. Barrmill is a very small village which boasted a rather fine station building, beside which a Bristol/ECW railbus stands with the 6.50 pm Lugton-Beith service on 5 May 1962. *W. A. C. Smith*

That building and all other evidence of the railway has gone, but on 18 June 1993 the background houses and the domestic power line pole still remained.

BARRMILL JUNCTION: Bristol/ECW railbus No SC79958, one of only two built, passes Barrmill Junction on its approach to Barrmill station to the left with the 12.45 pm Lugton-Beith service on 15 September 1962. The railbuses were really an early version of the modern 'Pacer' unit, their purpose being to reduce costs on lightly used branches, but even so they did not manage to prevent this branch from closure. *Douglas Hume*

By 24 July 1993 the G&SWR/Caley joint line from the junction to Beith has gone, but the Caley line from the former Barrmill Junction to Giffen survives as far as the Royal Navy Ammunition Dump at Giffen, albeit seeing very little traffic. The trees in the background have not changed much and amazingly the brick-built lineside hut remains to this day.

DALRY: Standard Class '5' No 73122 approaches Dalry with southbound coal empties on 11 September 1959.
Gavin W. Morrison

On 18 June 1993, under a leaden sky, Class '47' No 47146 heads north with a train of Tiphook Ferrywagons. As can be seen from this view, there is now a much simplified track layout with only two tracks and no sidings. The station platforms were also shortened in the re-modelling. The pole route has gone, but overhead catenary has been erected as part of the Ayr electrification. The Roche chemical plant in the background is rail connected and produces a weekly freight.

LOCHSIDE (1): Fairburn 2-6-4T No 42124 arrives at the station with the 5.33 pm Glasgow (St Enoch)-Kilmarnock via Dalry train on 25 June 1955. A solitary passenger is waiting. Lochside was on the line from Paisley to Dalry which passed to the east of Castle Semple Loch. There was also a line to the west of the loch which went through Lochwinnoch station. *W. A. C. Smith*

The west line is now closed and lifted and Lochside station has been renamed Lochwinnoch. As can be seen from the 18 June 1993 picture, it now forms part of the Glasgow-Ayr electrified route, as EMU No 318259 rushes through with the 09.00 from Glasgow. The footbridge has gone and the road bridge rebuilt to accommodate the overhead wires. Part of the stone wall remains on the southbound (up) platform.

LOCHSIDE (2): Standing on the roadbridge looking south, we see 'Black Five' No 44881 heading north with a freight on 25 June 1955. *W. A. C. Smith*

The same location on 18 June 1993 sees EMU No 318267 entering the station with a service for Glasgow (Central). Apart from the overhead wiring, the major change has been the removal of all the station buildings; the substantial main building has been replaced with a 'bus shelter'. The siding behind the up platform has also gone.

ELDERSLIE: 'Now you see it - now you don't!' The 'past' picture depicts Stanier Class '5' No 44790 passing through the station with a Glasgow (St Enoch)-Ayr relief on 14 May 1966. At that time all four platforms were in use, and the covered walkway from the station building to the road can clearly be seen on the right-hand side of the picture. To the west of the station was a junction where the lines to Greenock via Kilmacolm, and to Dalry via Lochwinnoch, left the main line, which was the Dalry via Lochside route. To the east of the station was Canal Junction at which point the loop through Paisley West and Paisley Canal left the main line which passed through Paisley Gilmour Street (see the map on page 136). *Fred Landery*

The present picture shows a complete transformation; the station has gone, as have the aforementioned junctions, leaving only the electrified main line from Glasgow to Ayr. A Class '318' EMU is seen heading for Glasgow. The electricity pylon is the one feature linking the two pictures.

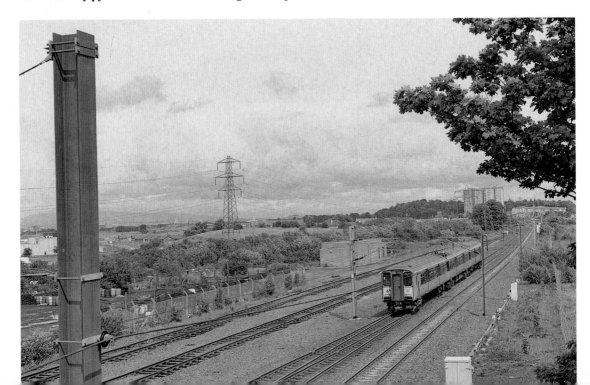

WEMYSS BAY is the splendid terminus at the end of the Caley line along the south bank of the Clyde, seen here in July 1969. The railway came to Wemyss Bay on 13 May 1865, the main purpose of extending the line thence from Greenock being to provide train connections for the Clyde steamers, with Rothesay being the principal destination. After an indifferent start, business picked up and remained buoyant right through to the early 1960s when passengers started to arrive by car and crossed to Rothesay by car ferry. The writer can well remember a family holiday in Rothesay in the late 1950s; on arriving at Wemyss Bay station from Glasgow (Central), a solid mass of people was slowly edging from the station on to the pier where the Rothesay-bound steamers were waiting. Being Glasgow Fair Saturday, trains were arriving every few minutes to disgorge more passengers, and shortly after arriving they would depart back to Glasgow to pick up yet more. This frantic scenario would last all morning, but would quieten considerably by the afternoon. The magnificent interior ironwork and superb awnings of the station are clearly in evidence. *David A. Anderson*

The present day picture shows the still magnificent structure, but sadly only a single platform is now in use. The access to the ferries is down the ramp behind the photographer. Happily, the station was being renovated when visited on 18 June 1993 and this necessitated a slightly different viewpoint. The booking office has been used to test out different colour schemes, hence the variety of tones which can be seen.

GREENOCK PRINCES PIER (1) opened for business on 25 May 1894 as the terminus of the Paisley, Bridge of Weir and Kilmacolm line. Much of the traffic for a while was in the shape of commuters from the Clyde coast towns of Rothesay and Dunoon making their way up to Glasgow via the ferries. The problem was that the same journey could be made by three different routes, by steamer to connect with trains at either Craigendoran, Gourock or at Princes Pier! The Second World War, then Nationalisation, brought an end to the steamers, but the Glasgow ser-

vice survived. During the 1950s and the early '60s ocean liners from the USA and Canada called at Princes Pier and special boat trains were run in connection with these arrivals. Fairburn 2-6-4T No 42190 waits at Princes Pier with the 2.20 pm (SO) for Glasgow on 22 June 1957. *Brian Morrison*

The passenger service to the pier was withdrawn on 14 February 1966 and freight services a few months later. The present scene, recorded on 1 August 1993, shows all trace of the railway swept away. The site is now a vast container depot, and thanks are due to the security guards at Greenock Ocean Terminal for allowing access to obtain the picture. Containers on lorries and ships seem to thrive, but not on railways!

GREENOCK PRINCES PIER (2): A superb gantry of semaphore signals guards the approach to Princes Pier station on 22 June 1957 as Pickersgill '3P' 4-4-0 No 54468 of Greenock Ladyburn shed (66D) shunts empty coaching stock outside the station. *Brian Morrison*

The exact viewpoint of the 'past' picture could not be replicated as it was in a secure compound for new cars. A telephoto lens was used to try and capture the salient features; the girders of the bridge over the Gourock road, to the left of the van, can also be seen alongside the second coach in the 'past' picture. A dramatic change over the years!

LANGBANK: For once one is grateful for road traffic in a railway picture! At this point the railway runs alongside the River Clyde, and on the far side of the river can be seen the outskirts of the town of Dumbarton. A BR Standard 2-6-4T heads the 12.15 pm Gourock-Glasgow (Central) service on 19 April 1965, while in the foreground is a superb selection of road vehicles which includes a Foden sugar tanker, a Wolseley, an Austin A55 van and a couple of Vauxhalls. *J. C. Beckett*

The railway scene is little changed apart from the electrification. The major change, however, is the construction of the M8 motorway on the land between the railway and the river. Owing to the verdant tree growth on the roadside the picture had to be taken further away from the girder bridge and shows EMU No 303013 on 18 June 1993 with a train for Glasgow. The distinctively shaped buoy still acts as a prominent marker for shipping.

PAISLEY ABERCORN: To the east of Paisley Gilmour Street station was Arkleston Junction from where a line ran to Renfrew Wharf. The line was originally built as a 4 ft 6 in guage line and opened on 3 April 1837 as the Paisley & Renfrew Railway. The line was purchased by the G&SWR on 31 July 1852 and converted to standard gauge in early 1866, re-opening for business on 1 May of that year. The junction signal is in the distance of this view of Highland Railway 'Jones Goods' No 103 and Caley 'Single' No 123 taking empty stock up to Renfrew Wharf on 14 September 1959 in connection with the Scottish Industrial Exhibition. The unusual feature is that the stock is coupled in front of No 123. This was extremely rare as there is a thistle engraved on each buffer and nothing was allowed to damage them (see also page 129). *S. C. Nash*

The present picture on 18 June 1993 shows that all trace of the railway has gone. The passenger service to Renfrew Wharf ceased on 5 June 1967 and nature has taken over with a vengeance, although there is a path along the trackbed amongst all the bushes and trees. The old 'prefabs' have also gone and have been replaced by modern housing, unfortunately hidden by the trees. Part of the stone wall still exists and can be seen on the extreme left.

RENFREW WHARF: The River Clyde can just be glimpsed beyond the bufferstops at the rear of the train, the houses and power station being on the opposite bank. With the large crane on the left, the picture illustrates the atmosphere of industrial Britain. Standard Class '4' No 76091 waits to depart with the 7.13 am to Glasgow (St Enoch) on 15 June 1963. *Douglas Hume*

Today the railway is but history, as is the power station, but the houses have survived and the site is in use as a chemical plant. The old Nissen hut on the right of the past picture has gone but has been replaced by one further away.

Lanarkshire lines

SYMINGTON: 'Crab' 2-6-0 No 42737 heads a railtour on 29 March 1964, having just left the West Coast Main Line and heading for Biggar, Broughton and eventually Peebles. Note the photographer's Ford Classic parked on the roadside and the elegant Caledonian signal. *Rodney Lissenden*

The scene on 23 May 1993 presents a very different picture. All trace of the railway has gone and the bushes now hide the road and house, but just look how the conifers have grown in the intervening 29 years! Amazingly the old fence on the right is still there.

BROUGHTON: No 42737 stands at Broughton station with the railtour of 29 March 1964. Broughton was situated almost midway between Symington Junction on the West Coast Main Line and the Caledonian station at Peebles (see 'British Railways Past and Present' No 9). The route opened to Broughton on 5 November 1860 and closed on 4 April 1966, although scheduled passenger trains had not run for many years prior to closure. *Rodney Lissenden*

By 23 May 1993 all trace of the station seemed to have disappeared. However, hidden behind the pile of pallets in the left foreground is the ramp of the south platform. A small industrial complex now occupies the site.

CARNWATH: The Caledonian Railway built a line from Carstairs to Edinburgh and the first station along the line was Carnwath. Class '5' No 45030 stands in the station with the 1.20 pm Edinburgh (Princes Street)-Lanark train on 15 April 1961. At this time No 45030 was allocated to Dalry Road shed (64C). *W. A. C. Smith*

Looking at the same view on 23 May 1993 the station and goods yard have gone completely, the site of the latter now a Strathclyde Regional Council Roads Depot. The line has been electrified and as a result electric trains coming up the West Coast from the south can run directly to Edinburgh without the need to change traction at Carstairs. A seven-coach buffer-fitted West of England HST set is seen heading south with the 11.05 from Edinburgh to Penzance.

SMYLLUM JUNCTION EAST: Looking north on 12 September 1959, we see Caley 'Single' No 123 and Highland Railway No 103 pass the signal box with empty coaching stock from Glasgow. Note the thistles engraved on the buffers of No 123 (see also page 124). The train has left the main line at Lanark Junction and has taken the left fork here to run to Smyllum Junction South. It will then reverse the stock along the third side of the triangle, past Smyllum Junction West and into Lanark station. The Smyllum Junctions were also known as the Douglas Junctions as the line to the south eventually passed Douglas. The sidings seen on the right were used for receiving trains of oil shale from West Lothian, and the adjacent factory, known as 'The Paraffin', extracted the oil. *S. C. Nash*

On 23 May 1993 there is a much changed scene. Only a single electrified line to Lanark remains for the hourly EMU service to Glasgow. The junctions and other lines have all gone.

LANARK: A single line from Lanark Junction to Lanark station was opened on 5 January 1855. The line was then doubled and extended to Douglas, opening on 1 April 1864. On 1 January 1873 it opened for goods traffic as far as Muirkirk, where this Caledonian line joined up with the G&SWR line from Auchinleck; it opened for passenger traffic on 1 June 1874. In 1923 a trade dispute in Muirkirk began a decline and the line eventually closed. Here we see contrasts at Lanark station on 12 September 1959; on the right is a Metro-Cammell DMU on a scheduled service, while on the left Caley No 123 and the 'Jones Goods' wait to depart with the 10.40 am special to Kelvin Hall in Glasgow. *S. C. Nash*

All that is left today is the electrified single line from Lanark Junction to Lanark station. On 31 May 1993 EMU No 314209 departs for Glasgow (Central). The church visible in the background of the 'past' picture has been demolished, but the large building on the left survives, as does the distinctive building on the right, although without its chimneys.

HAMILTON MPD (66C) was mainly a freight depot with an allocation of around 50 locos in steam days. By 1960 a large part of the shed was given over to DMUs, and this picture, taken on 2 April 1961, shows three railbuses (the two Bristol/ECW units with a Park Royal unit between them) parked outside the shed. The last of the steam locos went in 1962. *Noel A. Machell*

On 31 July 1993 there is nothing to suggest there once was an engine shed on this site, with an adjacent foundry. The picture was taken at the former entrance to the shed yard. The line from Hamilton West to Glasgow via Newton Junction is, however, still operational, out of sight to the right.

FERNIEGAIR JUNCTION: On 9 July 1960 Standard Class '4MT' No 76002 comes off the Ross Junction-Ferniegair Junction goods line with an Orange Walk special from Motherwell to Larkhall (East), the latter station having been re-opened for the occasion. On the right Standard 2-6-4T No 80057 waits at signals on the Haughead Junction (Hamilton)-Ferniegair Junction connection with a special from Glasgow (Central) to Larkhall (Central) via Hamilton. *W. A. C. Smith*

Today there is no indication that this was ever a railway. The houses and Ferniegair Mission Church still remain but are hidden by the trees. The electricity posts and power line are the only linking items in the pictures.

STONEHOUSE station can be seen in the background as a Derby built three-car DMU leaves for Coalburn on the 5.11 pm service from Glasgow (Central). The train to form the connection to Strathaven is still in the station. *Fred Landery*

The situation on 17 June 1993 is that road is again preparing to take over from rail. The line closed on 4 October 1965 and the trackbed was left to nature, but now the earthmovers are preparing it to form the Stonehouse Bypass. Over the years the scenery has changed little apart from a new building in front of the house in the background.

STRATHAVEN: 2-6-4T No 42125 approaches Strathaven Junction and the Central station with the 10.50 am from Maryhill, Glasgow, on 14 April 1962; the train is on the line from Stonehouse. The line on the higher viaduct came south from High Blantyre then curved sharply right and dropped down on to the viaduct where it met up with the Stonehouse line before entering the Central station. A spur off the High Blantyre line ran to Strathaven North station. The line from Stonehouse closed to passengers on 4 October 1965. *W. A. C. Smith*

The present-day picture was taken on 23 May 1993, and only the house on the hill is identifiable from the earlier picture; the other buildings are all obscured by trees. The two viaducts have been completely demolished, although the embankment which carried the higher line can still be identified. However, without the two viaducts it is a much changed scene.

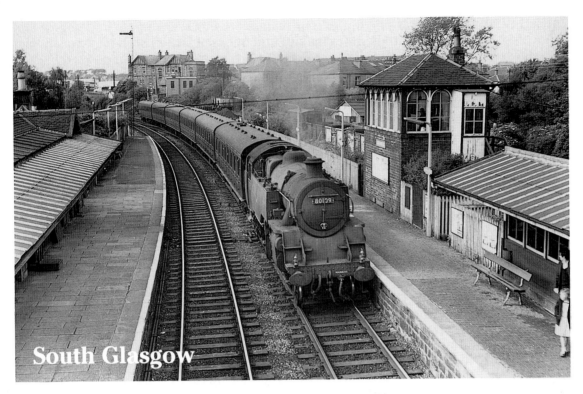

South Glasgow

GIFFNOCK: This is the station as it was on 18 June 1964, complete with the signal box on the platform, as Standard 2-6-4T No 80109 heads the 5.33 pm Glasgow (St Enoch)-East Kilbride commuter train into the platform. *Douglas Hume*

On 24 July 1993 we find all the buildings on the down platform have gone, along with the goods yard. The buildings on the up side have been rebuilt and a large car park provided. The large house in the background is now more obscured by trees as 'Sprinter' No 156508 pulls in with an East Kilbride service.

Corkerhill MPD (67A) was one of the four main motive power depots in Glasgow and its locomotives were used to haul trains into and out of St Enoch station. It was in fact the largest engine shed on the Glasgow & South Western Railway, and opened in 1896 partly to help out the shed at St Enoch which was cramped and awkwardly placed. With the opening of the new shed, some three miles from Glasgow city centre, there was also a custom-built village of terraced houses for the railway workers. The village soon boasted a population of over 700 people, and it survived until the 1950s when the houses were demolished and local authority houses, mainly flats, were built in their place.

With the closure of St Enoch shed in 1935, all locos serving St Enoch station were concentrated on Corkerhill. The depot's allocation of locos was primarily for passenger work, mainly to the Clyde coast but also to Stranraer, Dumfries and Carlisle. The shed had a large allocation of around 90 steam locos, with the pride of the shed being the handful of 'Jubilee' 4-6-0s.

Following the introduction of the Standard classes of locomotives, Corkerhill received a fair selection of Class '5s' (73000s), Class '4s' (76000s), Class '4' tanks (80000s) and a '2MT' 2-6-0, No 78026.

The last steam working from Corkerhill was in April 1967, although an occasional engine from Carlisle Kingmoor visited the shed after this date. Today the depot is as busy as ever servicing DMUs and EMUs in its modern facilities.

Finally, the authors would like to thank Thomas Boag, Train Crew Supervisor at Corkerhill, for identifying the exact locations of the following Corkerhill 'past' pictures. Without his help it is doubtful if the 'present' pictures could have been taken, such has been the transformation.

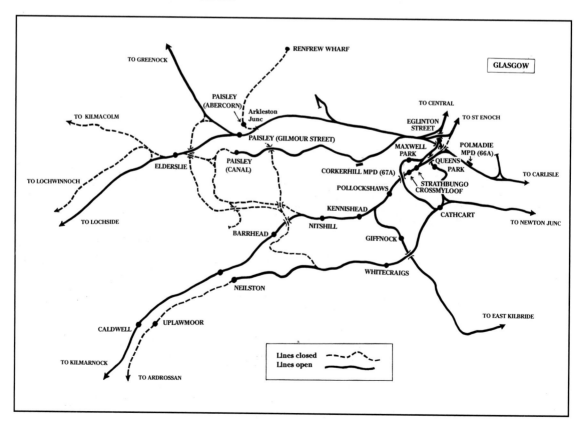

CORKERHILL MPD (1): A distinguished visitor to 67A on 18 April 1965 was Highland Railway 4-6-0 No 103, otherwise known as the 'Jones Goods', seen here posing in the sun at the west end of the shed. *Noel A. Machell*
   The present view shows that the Nissen hut has gone and the tracks have been realigned, but the background is still much the same.

CORKERHILL MPD (2): 'Black Five' No 45171 stands outside the maintenance shed on 16 September 1962.
Noel A. Machell

The maintenance shed line has not been altered but the shed has been demolished; Class '101' DMU No 101864 stands over the inspection pit which used to be inside the building. Behind the row of EMUs is the line to Paisley (Canal) which re-opened to passenger services on 30 November 1992.

CORKERHILL MPD (3): On 18 April 1965 Standard '4MT' tank No 80025 and Standard '5MT' 4-6-0 No 73102 rest between duties. They are standing on road 6A alongside the south-western corner of the main shed building. Note the distinctive smoke outlets and roof, all constructed from corrugated steel. *Noel A. Machell*

As we have seen, the old shed has been demolished and a new maintenance shed has been built over part of the site occupied by the old building. The tracks have also all been relaid.

CORKERHILL MPD (4): A line-up of stored ex-Caley and ex-LMS engines stand alongside the coaling plant on 2 April 1961. The coaling plant was one of the largest in the country and had a capacity of 300 tons in two vast bunkers. *Noel A. Machell*

The view of the south-eastern corner of the shed shows all evidence of the steam age gone and instead much realigned trackwork with all roads now electrified.

CATHCART (1): The 8.49 am Uplawmoor-Glasgow (Central) train is seen arriving at the station on the morning of 13 May 1961. Already the wires are in place for the electrification of the suburban system, but Fairburn tank No 42057 of Polmadie MPD is still in reasonable condition. *Michael Mensing*

EMU No 303004 is seen entering the station on 31 July 1993. Apart from the traction and the tree growth there has been no change at all.

CATHCART (2): Turning round to look north into the station, we see the Cathcart circle as it was on 12 September 1961 with a Derby Lightweight DMU set forming an outer circle train - this would travel out via Queens Park and return via Maxwell Park. *Michael Mensing*

Thirty-two years later and one of the 'Blue trains', No 303013, arrives at Cathcart station with a service for Neilston, having come via Queens Park. This EMU is old enough to have been in the past picture, having been built in 1960. When first introduced they were in a very attractive blue livery, hence the 'Blue train' tag. Unit No 303048 has been restored to this livery and is used on special occasions. The old semaphore has been replaced by a colour light and an awning has been added to the end of the platform building, but that apart there has been almost no change.

CATHCART WEST JUNCTION on 21 April 1960, with Standard Class '4' 'Mogul' No 76094 pulling away from Cathcart station across the junction with the 5.57 pm service from Glasgow (Central) to Whitecraigs on the Neilston line. *W. A. C. Smith*

EMU No 303032 passes the junction with a Neilston train on 31 July 1993. The lines diverging to the right behind the first coach in the 1960 picture have gone, as has the signal box at the junction, and the lines are now electrified. The old tenements on the main road are still standing, albeit partially hidden by newer properties.

INDEX OF LOCATIONS